# HOW TO MEASURE LIGHT

**LIGHT AS ENERGY | ENCYCLOPEDIA KIDS BOOKS | SCIENCE GRADE 5 | CHILDREN'S PHYSICS BOOKS**

**BABY PROFESSOR**

EDUCATION KIDS

First Edition, 2021

Published in the United States by Speedy Publishing LLC, 40 E Main Street, Newark, Delaware 19711 USA.

© 2021 Baby Professor Books, an imprint of Speedy Publishing LLC

Baby Professor Books are available at special discounts when purchased in bulk for industrial and sales-promotional use. For details contact our Special Sales Team at Speedy Publishing LLC, 40 E Main Street, Newark, Delaware 19711 USA. Telephone (888) 248-4521 Fax: (210) 519-4043.

10 9 8 7 6 * 5 4 3 2 1

Print Edition: 9781541949386
Digital Edition: 9781541951181
Hardcover Edition: 9781541983885

*See the world in pictures. Build your knowledge in style.*
*www.speedypublishing.com*

# TABLE OF CONTENTS

MODERN XRAY MACHINE

MICROWAVE OVEN

What does an x-ray have in common with a microwave? They are examples of electromagnetic waves! This book will talk about light waves and other types of waves. It will explain the properties of waves and how they can be measured.

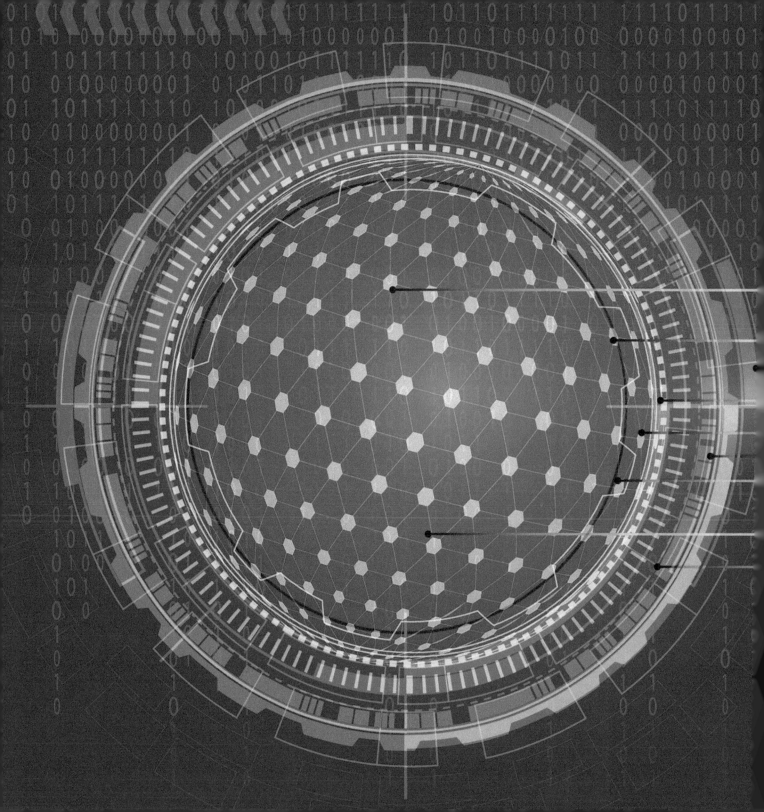

# CHAPTER ONE

# WAVES OF THE ELECTROMAGNETIC SPECTRUM

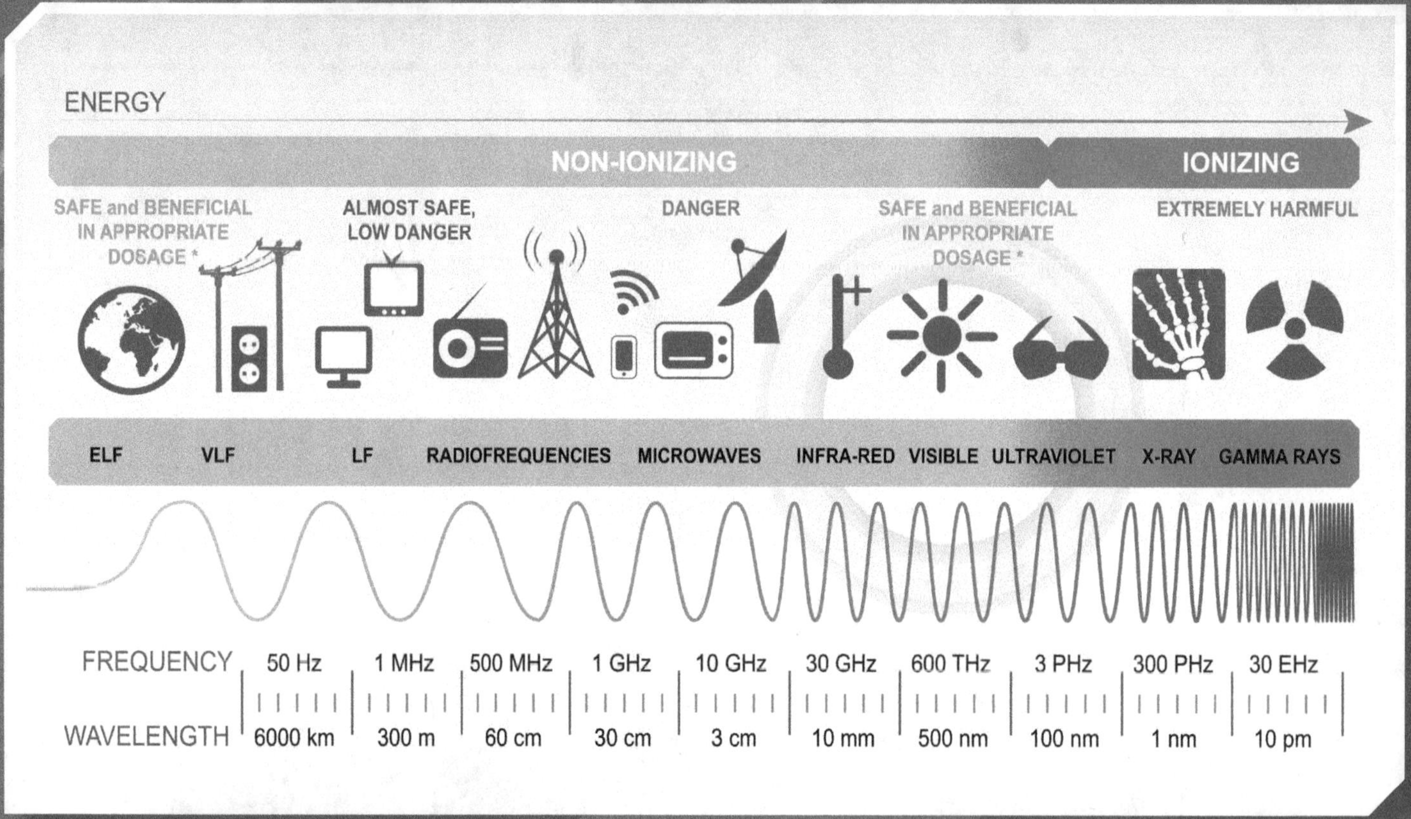


THE ELECTROMAGNETIC SPECTRUM

Light waves are a part of the electromagnetic spectrum. A spectrum means a range. The electromagnetic spectrum shows the range of the types of radiation. Radiation is an energy that travels and spreads. The light that we can see, visible light, is just one part of that spectrum. Electromagnetic just means that the radiation is both electric and magnetic. This chapter will teach you what light is, how we see, and other types of electromagnetic radiation.

## WHAT IS A LIGHT WAVE?

Light moves in waves. You can picture these waves like ocean waves. Another way to picture waves is if you shake the end of a rope. The rope will move upwards and downwards in a wave-like fashion.

Light is unique in that it is not only made of waves, but it is also made of small particles called photons. This is important because it allows light to travel even in a vacuum like in Space. A vacuum is a place where there is absolutely nothing.

ANOTHER WAY TO PICTURE WAVES IS IF YOU SHAKE THE END OF A ROPE. THE ROPE WILL MOVE UPWARDS AND DOWNWARDS IN A WAVE-LIKE FASHION.

PICTURE THROWING A PEBBLE INTO A LAKE. IT CAUSES RIPPLES.

Picture throwing a pebble into a lake. It causes ripples. These little waves are only possible because there is a medium, water, to carry them. That is why sound waves cannot travel in a vacuum. There is no medium. Light can travel in a vacuum because while it moves in waves, it also is made up of photons. These particles are so small that we cannot see them with the naked eye.

## VISIBLE LIGHT WAVES:

Visible light waves are the light waves that we can see. There are cones in our eyes that are sensitive to certain wavelengths. These cones allow us to see the visible light spectrum. There are other wavelengths that we simply cannot see. We must use special instruments to detect the other wavelengths that we cannot see.

When all the wavelengths of the visible spectrum combine, they form what we see as white light. It is only when the wavelengths are separated that we can see distinct colors.

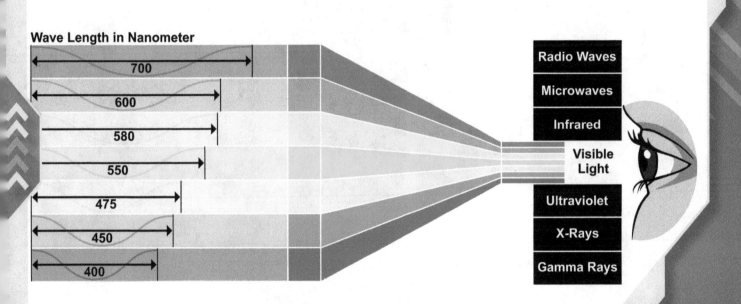

**Wave Length in Nanometer**

700
600
580
550
475
450
400

Radio Waves
Microwaves
Infrared
Visible Light
Ultraviolet
X-Rays
Gamma Rays

VISIBLE LIGHT WAVES ARE THE LIGHT WAVES THAT WE CAN SEE.

CUBIC PRISMS THAT REFRACT LIGHT AND
DIVIDE IT INTO A COLOR SPECTRUM

This can happen naturally. When light passes through water molecules in the air, it can cause the light to bend, or refract, separating out the different colors. These colors are red, orange, yellow, green, blue, indigo, and violet. In other words, this is how we see a rainbow. This can be seen artificially when light is passed through a prism.

Light waves reflect or bounce off objects which they hit. Since light moves so quickly, this reflection happens faster than we can see. When the light bounces back to us, we detect it through our eyes. It is then that we convert the information into images. The colors we see are based entirely on which wavelengths reflect.

COLORFUL MEXICAN CERAMIC JARS

# Absorption and Reflection

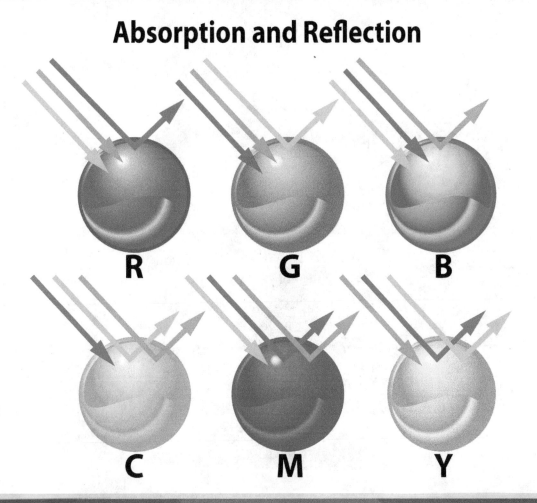

THE COLORS WE SEE ARE BASED ENTIRELY
ON WHICH WAVELENGTHS REFLECT.

TOMATOES APPEAR RED BECAUSE THE ONLY WAVELENGTH
OF LIGHT THAT THEY DO NOT ABSORB IS RED.

Darker colors absorb more light than lighter colors. Black absorbs all light; white reflects all light. Tomatoes, for instance, appear red. This is because the only wavelength of light that they do not absorb is red. What happens to this red light? The red light is reflected into our eyes.

**CMYK PROCESS COLORS – ABSORPTION AND REFLECTION**

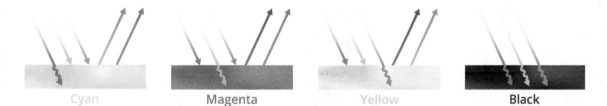

Cyan     Magenta     Yellow     Black

## TYPES OF WAVES:

The visible light spectrum is in the middle of the entire electromagnetic spectrum. The entire spectrum has a total of seven types of waves. The position of each of the waves in the spectrum depends on two things. Their size is the first thing, and the second thing is how quickly they move.

# ELECTROMAGNETIC SPECTRUM

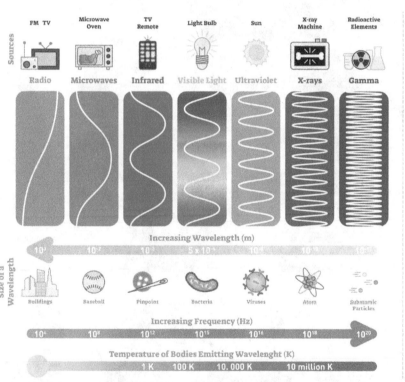

## ELECTROMAGNETIC WAVES

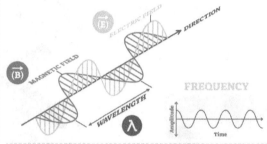

## VISIBLE SPECTRUM

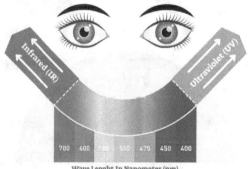

RADIO TOWER

Radio waves are known to have the longest waves. They can be used to send information. The music that you hear being played on the radio is sent on these waves. The information that is sent to a cellphone also depend on radio waves.

THE MUSIC THAT YOU HEAR BEING PLAYED ON THE RADIO IS SENT ON RADIO WAVES.

The next longest waves are microwaves. These are used to generate heat. This is why we call a microwave in the kitchen a microwave. We use microwaves to warm or even to cook our food.

WE USE MICROWAVES TO WARM OR EVEN TO COOK OUR FOOD.

MICROWAVE OVEN

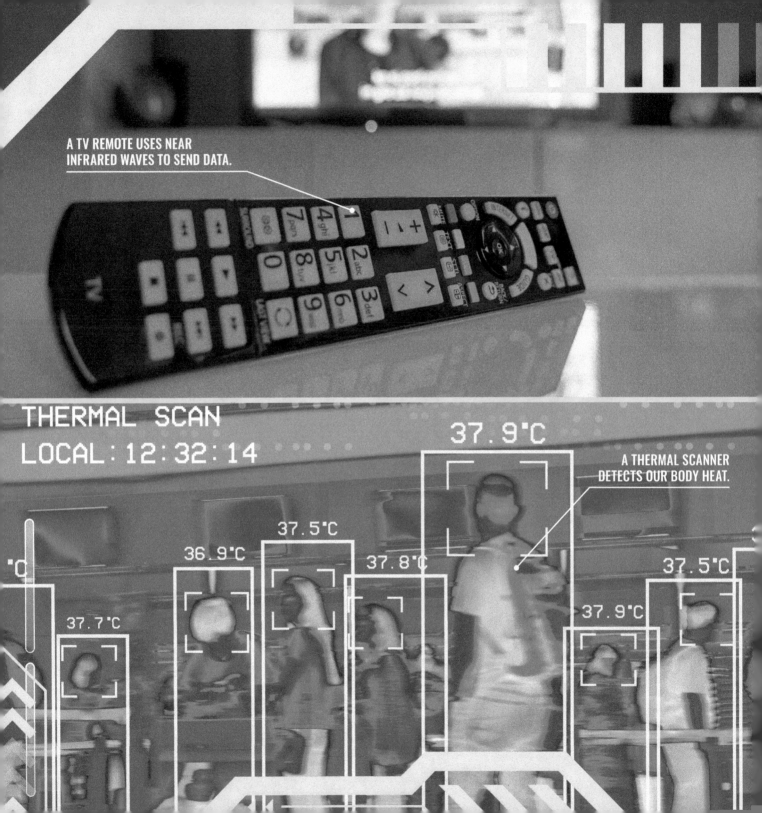

A TV REMOTE USES NEAR INFRARED WAVES TO SEND DATA.

THERMAL SCAN
LOCAL : 12:32:14

37.9°C

A THERMAL SCANNER DETECTS OUR BODY HEAT.

37.5°C

36.9°C

37.8°C

°C

37.7°C

37.9°C

37.5°C

Next there are infrared waves. Infrared waves are just below red light, and so are just outside our range of vision. There are two types of infrared waves: near and far. Near infrared waves can send data. They are the waves that allow a remote control to work. Far infrared rays though are what give off heat. Did you know that your body heat gives off infrared rays?

After visible light, of course, are the shorter, high energy waves. After violet, the last color that we can see, there is ultraviolet light. Ultraviolet light is in sunlight. This type of light helps plants to grow and it helps us make vitamin D. However, too much ultraviolet light can damage the skin which is why wearing sunscreen can be important.

LIGHT FROM THE SUN HELP PLANTS TO GROW AND IT HELPS US MAKE VITAMIN D.

ULTRAVIOLET LIGHT IS IN SUNLIGHT.

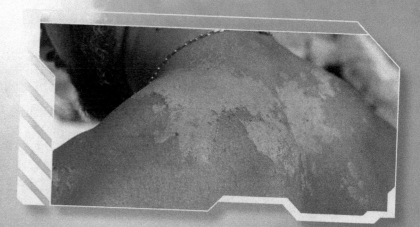

TOO MUCH ULTRAVIOLET LIGHT CAN DAMAGE THE SKIN.

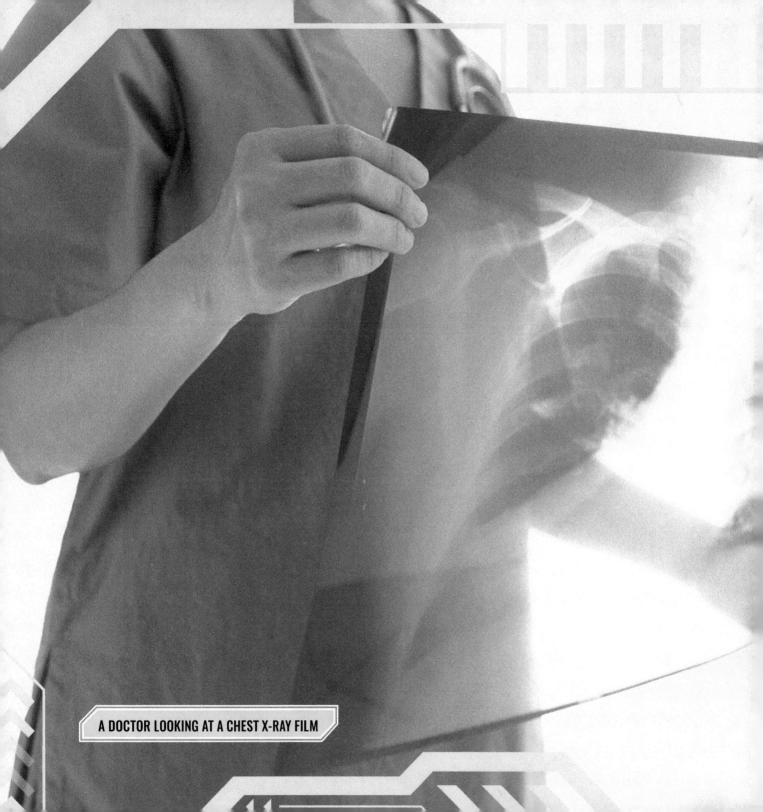

A DOCTOR LOOKING AT A CHEST X-RAY FILM

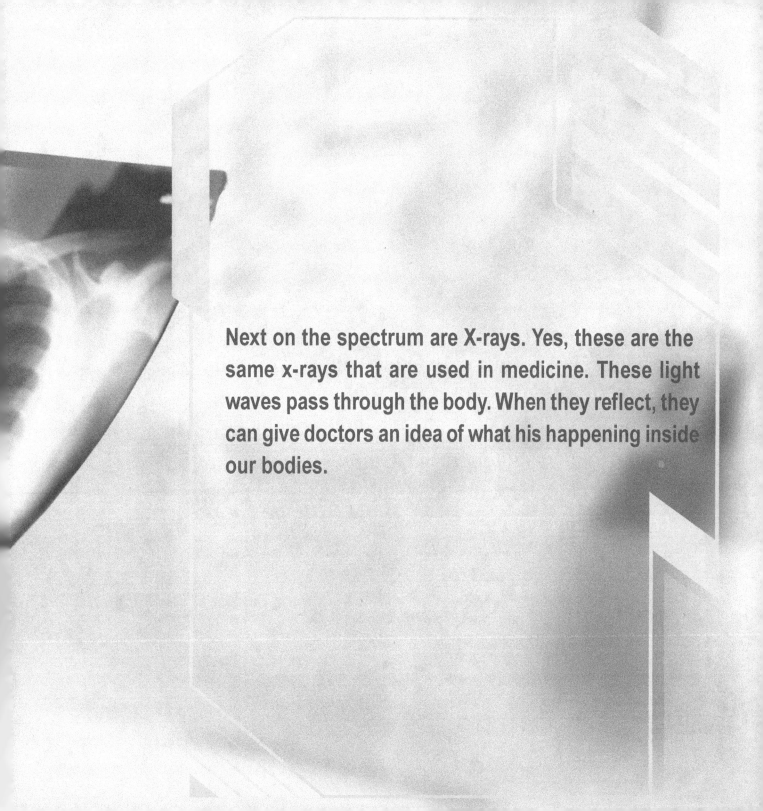

Next on the spectrum are X-rays. Yes, these are the same x-rays that are used in medicine. These light waves pass through the body. When they reflect, they can give doctors an idea of what his happening inside our bodies.

Gamma rays are the shortest of all the waves. They have a lot of energy. This energy can be used to kill cancer cells and to preserve food. Gamma rays can also be dangerous. They can be found around nuclear reactors, and they can be used to create atomic bombs.

NUCLEAR BOMB EXPLOSION

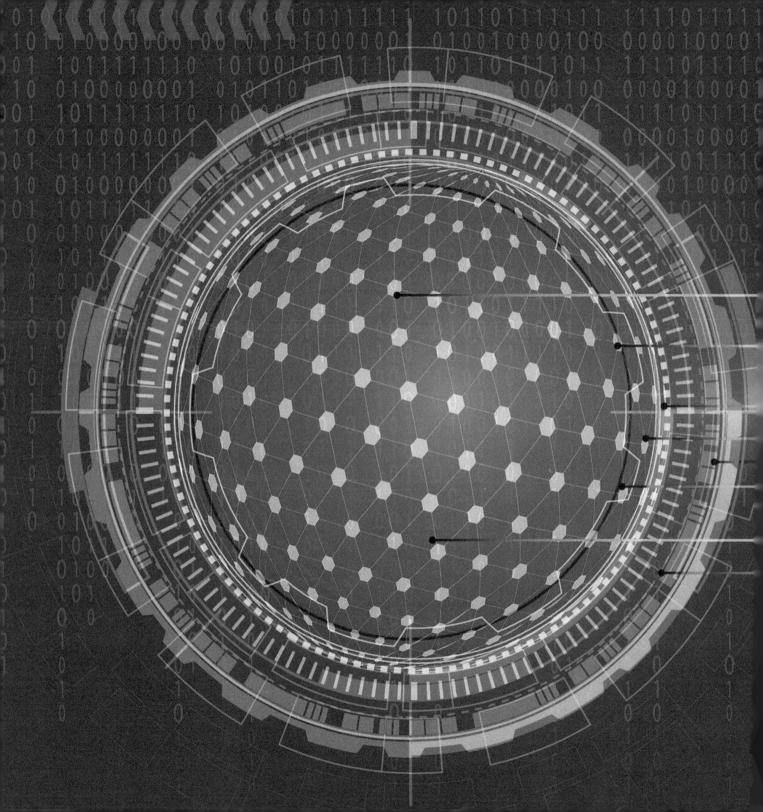

CHAPTER TWO

# HOW LIGHT IS MEASURED

**ELECTROMAGNETIC RADIATION MEASURING UNDER HIGH VOLTAGE POWER TRANSMISSION TOWERS**

In the last chapter, we learned that the electromagnetic spectrum is divided into different types. These types are based on how long the waves are and how much energy they have. This chapter will teach you all about how waves are measured.

## WAVELENGTH:

The length of a wave is measured from one crest to the next crest. The crest is the peak or top of the wave. In the visible light spectrum, red light, with approximately 30,000 waves for every inch, has the longest wavelength. Violet, on the other hand, has the shortest wavelength. It has 60,000 waves per inch.

IN THE VISIBLE LIGHT SPECTRUM, RED LIGHT, WITH APPROXIMATELY 30,000 WAVES FOR EVERY INCH, HAS THE LONGEST WAVELENGTH.

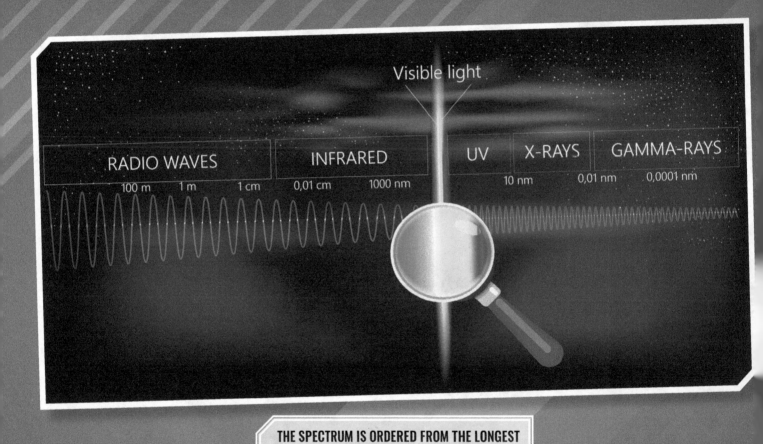

Visible light

RADIO WAVES | INFRARED | UV | X-RAYS | GAMMA-RAYS

100 m    1 m    1 cm    0,01 cm    1000 nm    10 nm    0,01 nm    0,0001 nm

THE SPECTRUM IS ORDERED FROM THE LONGEST
WAVELENGTH TO THE SHORTEST WAVELENGTH.

For the entire electromagnetic spectrum, radio waves would have the longest wavelength. Gamma rays have the shortest wave lengths. The spectrum is ordered from the longest wavelength to the shortest wavelength.

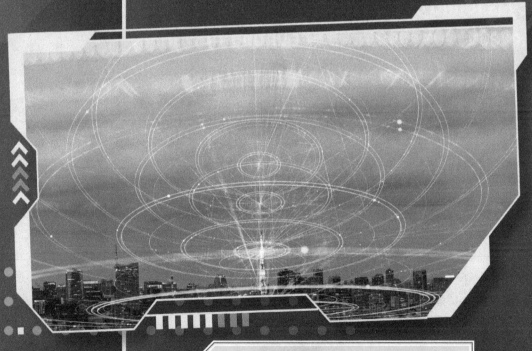

RADIO WAVES HAVE THE LONGEST WAVELENGTH

## FREQUENCY:

Frequency is found by measuring how quickly the waves move. It is measured by counting how many waves pass by a set point in a set period. The units of frequency are measured in cycles per second. If something has three cycles per second, this means that there were three waves that passed in a second.

# Frequency

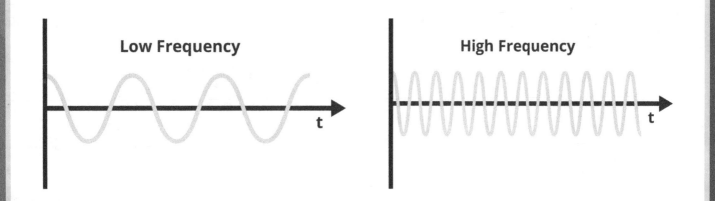

Low Frequency

High Frequency

t

t

FREQUENCY IS FOUND BY MEASURING
HOW QUICKLY THE WAVES MOVE.

WHEN YOU TUNE IN TO YOUR FAVORITE RADIO STATION, YOU TUNE IN TO A SPECIFIC FREQUENCY.

The different types of light can be divided as much by frequency as by wavelength. Do you have a radio station that you like to listen to? When you tune in to this radio station, you tune in to a specific frequency. Those radio waves are traveling at a certain speed.

You may have guessed that wavelength and frequency are related. Colors with longer wavelengths will have lower frequencies. On the other hand, colors with shorter wavelengths will have higher frequencies. When you think about it this way, it should make sense. Waves with longer wavelengths have more distance between the crests. This makes it harder for more waves to pass by in a second. If the wavelengths are shorter, they can move faster. This is also why we say shorter wavelengths, or higher frequencies, have more energy.

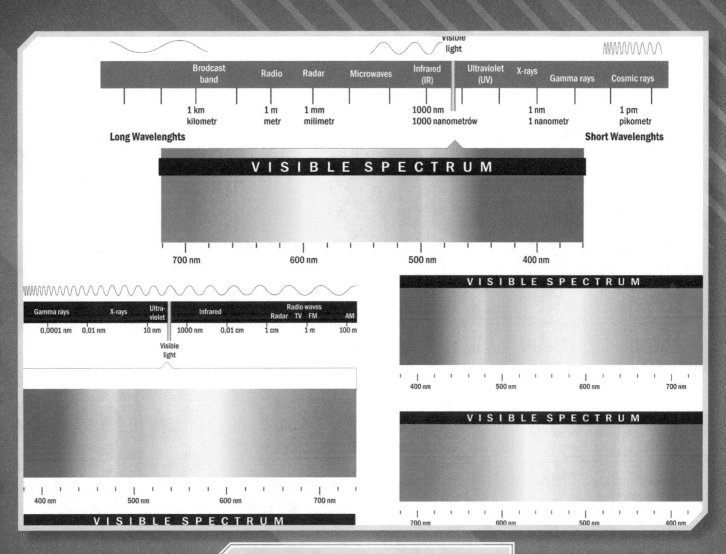

VISIBLE SPECTRUM - WAVELENGTH AND FREQUENCY

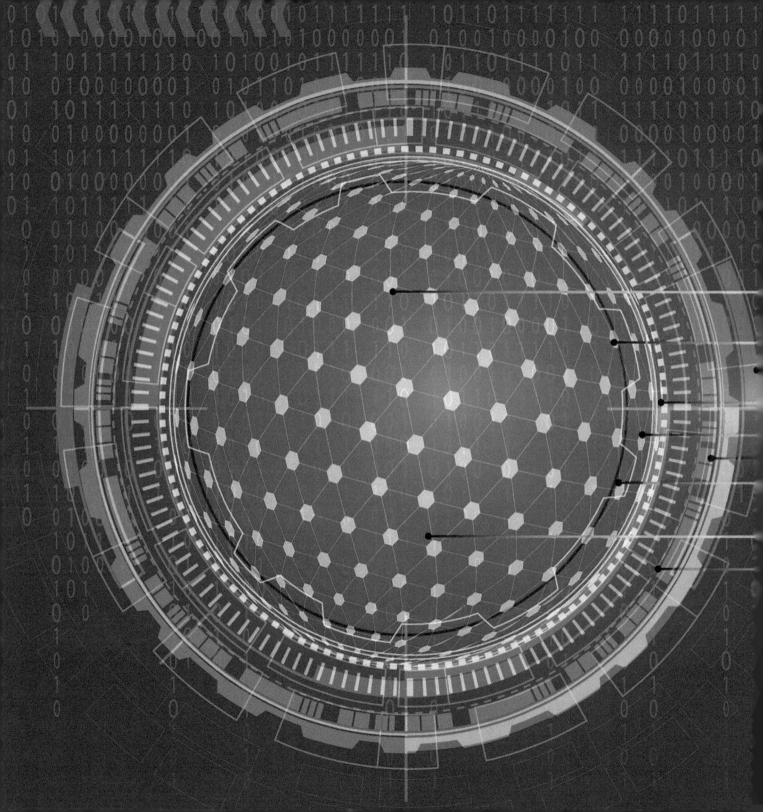

# CHAPTER THREE

# EXPERIMENTS

IT IS POSSIBLE TO TEST THE CONCEPTS MENTIONED
IN THIS BOOK BY TRYING A SIMPLE ACTIVITY
AND THEN A SIMPLE EXPERIMENT AT HOME.

It is possible to test the concepts mentioned in this book by trying a simple activity and then a simple experiment at home. This chapter will guide you through the activity and the experiment. The activity will show you how to count the frequency of waves. Then, the experiment will show how wavelengths and frequency are related.

## HOW TO COUNT THE FREQUENCY OF WAVES:

To begin the activity, fill a pan up with water and place it on a table or a counter. Wait until the water is completely still. When it is still, place your finger in the water and wait until the water is tranquil once more. Once it is, move your finder and observe the wave that you make. Keep moving your finger back and forth until you produce a continuous series of waves at the same wavelength. Count how many waves hit the edge of the pan in a minute. That is your frequency.

FILL A PAN UP WITH WATER AND PLACE IT ON A TABLE OR A COUNTER.

# HYPOTHESIS

AN EXPERIMENT IS A MEANS OF
TESTING IF WHAT YOU BELIEVE IS TRUE.

## AN EXPERIMENT TO TEST HOW CYCLES ARE AFFECTED BY WAVELENGTH:

An experiment is more than just an activity. It is a means of testing if what you believe is true. All experiments must have a hypothesis. A hypothesis is a statement about what you believe will happen. It must be specific and something you can disprove. In this case, your hypothesis will be that as the wavelength decreases, the frequency will increase.

The next thing to do will be to gather the materials you need for your experiment. For this experiment, get a paddle ball. (That is just a wooden paddle with a ball attached to it with elastic or string.) Also, get a piece of elastic or string, a stopwatch, and a pencil and paper.

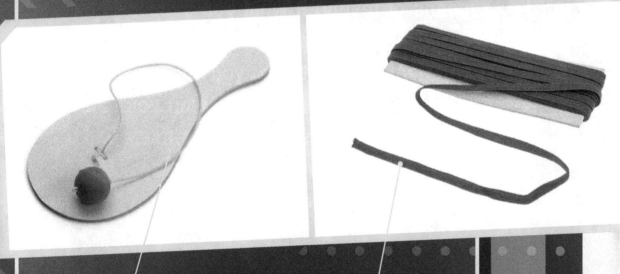

PADDLE BALL

STRING

STOPWATCH

SCIENTIFIC EXPERIMENTS SHOULD BE RECORDED DILIGENTLY.

Make certain that you write down everything you do, your hypothesis, the materials you use, your thoughts, observations, and procedures. Scientific experiments should be recorded diligently. That way other scientists can look over your results and repeat your experiment to get the same results. If they do not get the same results, either they or you will have done something wrong. In Science, the ability to repeat results is important. By confirming each other's results, it is easier to catch mistakes and find the truth.

## THE PROCEDURE AND RESULTS:

Bounce the ball at a steady rate for fifteen seconds. Count how many times you can hit the ball. Record your results.

Now shorten the cord attaching the ball to the paddle. Fold the cord in half and keep it together with your elastic or string. Now bounce the ball for another fifteen seconds and count how many times you hit the ball. Record your results.

BOUNCE THE BALL AT A STEADY RATE FOR FIFTEEN SECONDS.

By counting the number of times that you hit the ball, you were counting your cycles. The number of times you hit it in fifteen seconds is your frequency. The length of the cord is your wavelength. You should have noticed that when you shortened the wavelength, you were able to hit the ball more. There was less distance for the ball to travel to get back to you. In the same fashion, shorter wavelengths of light have higher frequencies.

In this case, your results should support your hypothesis. In Science, there is no shame in having an incorrect hypothesis. Learning what you believe is wrong is an important step on the journey for truth.

YOUR RESULTS SHOULD SUPPORT YOUR HYPOTHESIS.

LEARNING WHAT YOU BELIEVE IS WRONG IS AN IMPORTANT STEP ON THE JOURNEY FOR TRUTH.

THERE ARE DIFFERENT TYPES OF
ELECTROMAGNETIC WAVES.

There are different types of electromagnetic waves. A wave's size and its frequency determine where the wave is located on the electromagnetic spectrum.

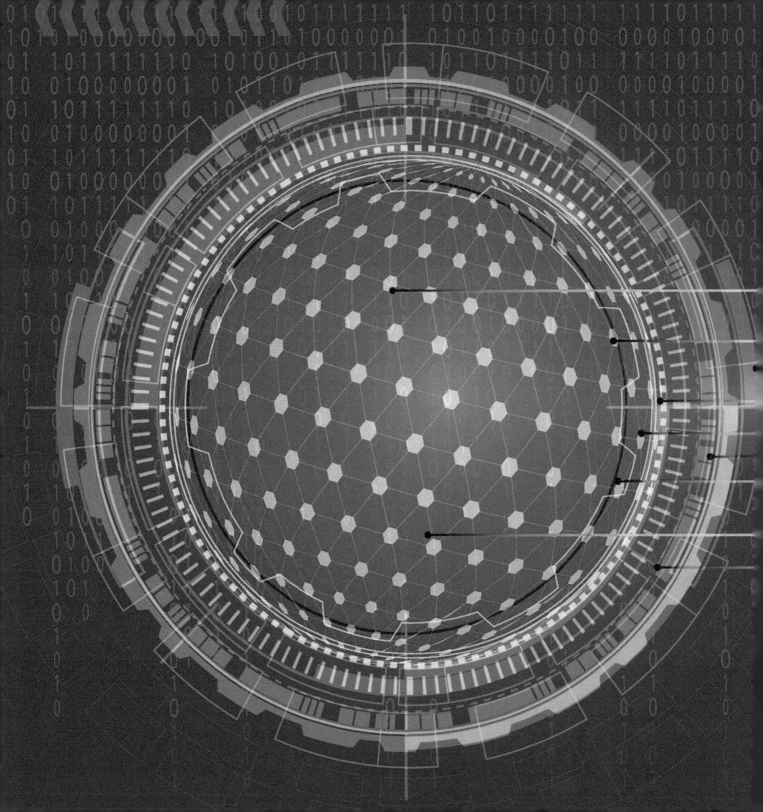

# VISIT

*www.speedypublishing.com*

To view and download free content on your
favorite subject and browse our catalog of new
and exciting books for readers of all ages.

CPSIA information can be obtained
at www.ICGtesting.com
Printed in the USA
BVHW011706181122
652290BV00023B/183